The Big Test

Written by
Rob Waring and **Maurice Jamall**

Before You Read

to fall
down

screen

to laugh

test

to sell
something

transmitter

library

video

school
nurse

hurt

In the story

Steve

Ryan

Mike

Mr. Harris

"Are you ready for the test?" asks Jenny. Everybody is studying in the library for tomorrow's test. Jenny and her boyfriend Alex are studying hard. They are worried about the test.
"No, I'm not ready," says Alex. "I hate tests!"
"Me too!" says Jenny. "I'm not going to be ready. I can't pass the test," she says sadly.

"Steve, why aren't you studying?" Alex asks. "Are you ready for the test?"

"Of course, I'm ready," he says. "I'm not worried. It'll be okay."

Alex says, "But you aren't studying! The test is tomorrow!"

"It's okay, we aren't worried," says Ryan. "We can pass the test."

"You're not studying. How can you pass the test?" asks Alex.
"Yes, how can you pass?" asks Jenny.
Ryan says, "It's our secret! We're not going to tell you."
"Yeah, it's our secret," says Steve.
They are smiling because they have a plan.

After lunch, Ryan and Steve are walking near Mr. Harris's room.
"Are you ready?" asks Steve.
"Yeah. Okay, let's do it!" says Ryan.
Ryan falls down near Mr. Harris's room.
"Ouch, my leg, it hurts," Ryan shouts. "I can't move! My leg!
Help! Help! Help!"
Steve is laughing. Ryan's leg is not hurt.

Mr. Harris comes out of his room. "What's wrong? What's happening?" he asks.
Steve says to Mr. Harris, "Please help, Mr. Harris. Ryan's hurt."
Ryan says, "Mr. Harris, I hurt my leg. Please help me."
"But your leg looks okay," says Mr. Harris.
Ryan's leg is okay. Steve and Ryan want Mr. Harris to leave his room.

Ryan says, "But Mr. Harris, my leg hurts. Please take me to the school nurse."

"Don't worry, Ryan. It's okay," says Mr. Harris.

He speaks to Steve. "Steve, take Ryan to the school nurse, please. Quickly!" he says.

"Sorry Mr. Harris, I can't. I have class now," Steve replies.

"Okay, Ryan. Come with me. I'll take
you," says Mr. Harris. "Are you okay?"
"No, not really. It hurts," says Ryan.
Mr. Harris takes Ryan to the school nurse.
Steve does not go to class. He watches
Mr. Harris and Ryan. He is smiling.

Steve waits for them to leave. Then he looks around. He has a plan.
He does not see anybody. "Good," he thinks. He goes into
Mr. Harris's room quietly. He does not want anybody to see him.
"Good," he thinks again. "The plan's working!"

Steve goes to the computer. He puts a transmitter into the back of the computer. The transmitter turns red.
"Good, it's working," he thinks. He smiles. "Our plan's working, too!"
Steve leaves the room quietly.

Later, Steve meets Ryan in the computer room.
"How's your leg?" asks Steve.
Ryan and Steve laugh. They know Ryan's leg does not hurt.
"Mr. Harris doesn't know. He thinks my leg hurts," says Ryan.
"Good job, Ryan!" says Steve.
"Did you put the transmitter in?" asks Ryan.

"Yeah, sure," says Steve.
Ryan asks, "Did anybody see you go into his room?"
"No," says Steve.
"Great! Is it working?" Ryan asks.
Steve says, "Of course. See!" He shows Ryan the
transmitter. Then he shows him the screen.

Mr. Harris is at the computer. The transmitter in the back of his computer is red. Now Ryan and Steve can see Mr. Harris's computer screen. Ryan and Steve both look at their screen. Mr. Harris is writing tomorrow's test. They can see Mr. Harris's test on their computer.

"Look," says Ryan. "There it is. It's the test! The plan worked!"

Steve and Ryan smile. They now have the test.
Ryan says, "Great job, Steve!"
"Let's go to the library to find the answers," says Ryan.
"And we can make some money, too."
Ryan and Steve go to the library. They find the answers
for the test.

Ryan sees his friend, Mike. "Do you want the answers for tomorrow's test?" he asks.

"Yeah, of course. How did you get the answers?" asks Mike.

Ryan says, "That's our secret." He shows the answers to Mike.

Mike asks, "What are the answers?"

"I'm not going to tell you. We want some money for them," says Ryan. Ryan and Steve get some money from Mike and some other boys, too.

The next day, everybody is worried about the big test.
Mr. Harris says, "Okay everybody. Let's start the test."
Ryan and Steve are not worried. They know the answers!
Mike smiles at Ryan. He knows the answers, too.
Mr. Harris gives the test to Mike and Ryan. He smiles when
he gives the test to Steve.
"Enjoy the test, Steve," Mr. Harris says.

Steve looks at the test. He is very surprised. It is a different test!

Steve says, "But Mr. Harris, this is not the same. . ."

Mr. Harris asks, "Excuse me, Steve, *what's* not the same?"

"Umm. . . nothing," Steve says.

Mr. Harris asks, "Steve do you want to say something?"

"Oh, Umm. . . No. . . Nothing," says Steve.

Mr. Harris smiles. "Then enjoy your test!" he says.

Steve looks at Ryan. Ryan looks at Steve.
"This is a new test," Steve says to Ryan, quietly. "Mr. Harris made a new test! It's different!"
"Yeah, I know! What happened?" asks Ryan.
"I don't know!" says Steve.
Mr. Harris is watching Steve and Ryan. He is smiling.

Steve looks at the test again.
"I can't do this test," he thinks. "I don't know the answers. Oh no!"
Steve tries to do the test. Mike and the other boys are angry with Ryan and Steve now.
"I'll speak to you later, Ryan!" Mike says to Ryan.

After the test Mike comes to Ryan. He is very angry.
Mike says, "That was a different test. I want my
money back."
"But I don't have your money!" says Ryan.
"What?" says Mike. "You don't have my money?
Ryan, give it to me tomorrow, or you're in big
trouble!" he says angrily.
"Okay, okay," says Ryan. "I'll give you the money
tomorrow."

Mr. Harris says, "Steve and Ryan, please come to my room now. I want to speak to you."
"Yes, Mr. Harris," they say.
"What is this about?" asks Steve.
"Wait and see," says Mr. Harris.
Ryan and Steve go with Mr. Harris to his room.

They go into Mr. Harris's room. They are worried.
"What do you want?" asks Steve.
"Sit down, please," he says. "I want you to see this."
Ryan looks at Steve.
"What is it?" they think. "What does Mr. Harris want
to show us?" They are very worried now.

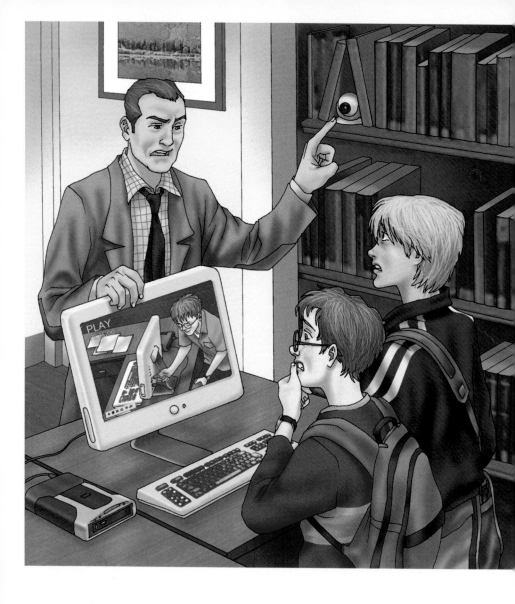

Mr. Harris shows them his computer. There is a video on the
screen. It is a video of Steve. Steve is putting something in
the back of the computer. Steve and Ryan are very shocked.
They are in big trouble now!